LEAD YOUR STAFF TO THINK LIKE EINSTEIN, CREATE LIKE DA VINCI, AND INVENT LIKE EDISON

52 Powerful Real-World Techniques that Work!

D1563267

LEAD YOUR STAFF TO THINK LIKE EINSTEIN, CREATE LIKE DA VINCI, AND INVENT LIKE EDISON

52 Powerful Real-World Techniques that Work!

DON BLOHOWIAK

IRWIN
Professional Publishing

Chicago • Bogotá • Boston • Buenos Aires • Caracas
London • Madrid • Mexico City • Sydney • Toronto

Senior sponsoring editor:	Cynthia A. Zigmund
Marketing manager:	Mary Ellen Roberts
Project editor:	Denise Santor-Mitzit
Production supervisor:	Pat Frederickson
Designer:	Laurie J. Entringer
Manager, graphics and desktop services:	Kim Meriwether
Compositor:	ElectraGraphics, Inc.
Cartoons:	Ken Wilke
Typeface:	11/14 Garamond
Printer:	Quebecor

Library of Congress Cataloging-in-Publication Data

Blohowiak, Donald W.
    Lead your staff to think like Einstein, create like Da Vinci, and
invent like Edison : 52 powerful real-world techniques that work ! /
Don Blohowiak.
      p.   cm.
    ISBN 0-7863-0424-3
    1. Creative ability in business. 2. Leadership. I. Title.
HD53.B57   1995
658.4'092—dc2094–44810

Printed in the United States of America
1 2 3 4 5 6 7 8 9 0 QF 2 1 0 9 8 7 6 5

For Doug, Mary Dell, Liz and Kate

PREFACE

If you manage at least one other person and are expected to produce more work in less time, with fewer resources, and at higher standards of quality, this book is for you. In 52 brief chapters—one for every week of the year—you'll find help for the awesome challenge of meeting ever-increasing expectations with ever-decreasing support from your organization.

The principles and methods described between these covers are based on *Mavericks!*, my 1992 book, which, through several foreign-language translations and growing worldwide sales, is finding acceptance around the globe. The positive media reviews and appreciative letters from readers in many countries confirmed that *Mavericks!* gave individual managers workable solutions to tough workplace challenges. This book distills many of those lessons, adds a few new ones, and presents them in a quick, palatable format.

I am grateful to the correspondents and reviewers who saw both promise and fulfillment in the ideas you are about to read. And I am especially grateful to the many bosses and employees I've been privileged to work with in my career. All have taught me the underlying and most profound principle that runs through every page of this book: **An individual manager's actions matter more than any organizational policy, period.**

Don Blohowiak
Princeton Junction, New Jersey

CONTENTS

CHAPTER 1

YOUR BEHAVIOR MATTERS MORE THAN TECHNIQUES

This book describes ways that you as a boss can influence the work of smart, talented people who think to make their living. Many management books imply that you need only issue a vision statement or publicly affirm warm feelings for the people on the payroll to have them magically perform to your expectations. Little is said about how you as the boss must behave to effect change in employee behavior.

The techniques described between these covers have more to do with how you spend your day as a boss than with the details of what you can do to your employees. The basic premise of this book is simple: *To manage a better staff, become a better manager.*

▌ WHERE DOES *MANAGEMENT* COME FROM?

Were you trained as a manager? You can become a boss with no preparation and not much more qualification. Many who assume authority over or responsibility for others do so ineffectively or even counterproductively. Organizations often reward and thus encourage harsh, even cruel, behavior by bosses whose methods result in short-term effects such as cutting costs, increasing profits, or boosting productivity.

You cannot obtain greatness from a person through threats, though for a short time fear can be an effective motivator to spur increased activity. Longer term, other methods are far more effective in encouraging improved performance among workers whose productivity depends on producing *thought-based* work, where attitude and motivation affect competence.

▌ MOTIVES MATTER MORE THAN METHODS

If you accept the idea that managers influence the work performance of the people who report to them, then it stands to reason that employees do better work when their managers are better prepared to help them. Tragically, formal management training usually teaches little about positively influencing people and scarcely anything about getting the best thinking or creativity—or even cooperation—from employees.

Most management literature and education seems obsessed with process improvement where the cure for vexing challenges is assumed to lie in defining evermore streamlined and efficient techniques. This mentality suggests that overcoming tough challenges merely requires the right tools. When applied to people, this principle has managers eternally chasing after hot techniques to tweak productivity from the payroll ("Five Easy Steps to Doubling Anyone's Workload").

No scientific method exists to get people to give an organization their best thinking, most creative ideas, and commitment of tireless energy. No methodology can squeeze inspired work from someone who does not want to give it.

A manager's approach to methods often matters more than the methods themselves. That's why people management programs that work marvelously well at one firm don't necessarily transfer well to another; the soul is lost in the transplant. Motive and action are inextricable. Your effectiveness as a manager comes from your influence as an ethical person who cares about the people you manage rather than the power of your position or the craftiness of your methods. When deployed with integrity, the methods described in this book will help people achieve their best. Without earnestness, they are hollow attempts to manipulate.

ACTION BIAS

For many of us, reading intriguing management material or attending seminars is similar to attending religious services. We clap our hands. We sing praises. We may even shout "hallelujah!" And as with religion, we often fail to grasp its greatest benefits because our emphasis is on belief, not practice. When the fleeting celebration is over, we go back into the world just as we did before.

Believing in managing better doesn't make you a better manager. That's why every one of the essays in this book concludes with a series of action steps. These actions are the tools of the **value-adding manager.** *Positive change begins with thinking new thoughts, but it happens by taking new actions.*

 ACTION STEPS

☐ Read this book with a commitment to improving your own performance.

☐ Write in your own action plans. Use the blank lines

to enrich the action steps that already are listed for you.

☐ _____

_____

_____

_____

CHAPTER 2

THE MOST IMPORTANT CORPORATE ASSET
WEIGHS THREE POUNDS AND IS INVISIBLE

In the new world competition, there are two strategies for beating your competitors. First you outthink them, then you outwork them. "Excellence" isn't enough. "Quality" isn't enough. Quality and excellence only buy you equilibrium with competent competitors; they do nothing to distinguish your organization from a cadre of customer-wooing competitors. To excel, you must create a corporate culture of constant innovation that ingrains ingenuity and high productivity into the workforce as today's work ethic.

THE CAPITAL THAT COUNTS

Flesh, blood, and brains, not buildings, turbines, or file servers, determine success. Computers and other machines fail to improve productivity or competitiveness at the point where human ingenuity and judgment must bear on the enterprise. The most advanced technology can't invent new products, generate innovative competitive strategies, or make customers feel welcome or served.

In our postindustrial world, it is not the capital assets or the number of employees that will determine a company's fate but rather the intensity of motivation and innovation of its work force. The most important corporate asset weighs only three pounds and is invisible to the unaided eye: the brain in every employee's head.

ACTION STEPS

☐ Examine your valuation of assets. Are you counting only depreciable physical assets?

☐ Honestly assess how your physical assets distinguish your organization from others with which you compete. Do they give you a sustainable competitive edge?

☐ Think how the unique knowledge and enlightened imagination of your workforce constitutes an irreplaceable and priceless asset.

☐ Review your investment strategy. Does "human capital" receive a regular and sufficient investment (money, time, priority) to upgrade it? Is your capital budget proportional to your skill development budget?

☐ _____

_____

_____

CHAPTER 3

IT'S NOT WHAT YOUR EMPLOYEES KNOW THAT
COUNTS, IT'S WHAT THEY IMAGINE

From supercomputers to tender chickens to increasing efficiency, ideas are the new currency of commerce: the new capital. The very word *capital* has its roots in the Latin *capitalis*, which means "relating to the head." So it is quite natural for capitalists to concentrate on the heady matters of creativity and innovation. With the Information Age now a reality, the creation of wealth truly is a creative activity.

Call it brain power, intellectual capital, creative assets, or whatever, thinking is the new competitive weapon. Business moves too fast for you ever to know what you need to know. So it's not just what people on your payroll know that counts, it's what they can imagine.

Creative people are not all painters or novelists anymore than all salespeople are universally gregarious or loquacious. Creative people can be found in all departments in an organization: finance, engineering, data processing, sales, research and development, operations, marketing, and human resources. The ability to generate original thinking has little to do with job function or even formal education.

Your job as a manager is to encourage more free thinkers—people who come up with ideas for improving products and processes without being told (or in spite of being told not to!).

"We're waiting to hear if it's okay to use the umbrellas!"

REVERSE YES MAN

When employees are not explicitly asked to contribute their thinking about issues and to challenge the organization's current conventions, a kind of "reverse yes man" mentality takes hold. Employees not only agree with the boss but censor themselves by sifting all their ideas through a filter of "will the boss buy this?"

The reverse yes man is most dangerous in an institution or work group that claims to value employee participation but offers no mechanism for it. Such an organization lies to itself: While it says it wants ideas from employees, nontraditional notions really aren't welcome. Employees instinctively grasp the gap between proclamation and reality. Innovative ideas never pass through the sieve of self-censorship.

The mortal enemy of fresh thinking in an organization is the bureaucrat-manager's inclination to codify, compartmentalize, and regulate highly prescribed procedures to paralysis. Such regimentation confines and controls most people, thereby assuring the controlling manager's monopoly on creative work that condemns everyone else to work without inspiration or psychic pleasure. People denied the joy of creativity in their work die a little inside. With no need to create, routine becomes monotony, then boredom, and, finally, living death.

No firm can afford mindless deference to organizational authority. Success demands innovative free thought on a large scale. As a value-adding manager and influencer of people, you wield tremendous power to turn loose the creative energy trapped and untapped in your colleagues.

 ACTION STEPS

☐ Create a *mechanism* for employees to contribute suggestions. Consider the time-honored suggestion box or its more contemporary equivalent, the electronic mailbox, dedicated to receiving tips, information, and recommendations.

☐ Allow and encourage anonymous suggestions. This will increase the volume of good ideas you receive.

Contrary to what many managers fear, the cloak of anonymity does not encourage mostly griping. Some people want to submit recommendations without their names attached because—despite your good intentions—they may fear reprisal. Others may merely want to improve their organization and have no need to receive credit for their ideas.

☐ Frequently remind your staff that you welcome, want, and need their ideas on how to make the enterprise more efficient, more productive, and more successful.

☐ Commit yourself to serious, timely consideration to all suggestions. Publish or post a listing of the ideas submitted and the actions you're taking on them. Explain why you are rejecting a suggestion.

☐ Encourage a culture of discovery. Ask yourself, and encourage everyone who works with you to ask:
　☐ What do we know?
　☐ What do we need to know?
　☐ What do we know we don't know?
　☐ What else is there to know?

☐ _____

_____

_____

CHAPTER 4

TIE PAYCHECK SIZE TO RESULTS DELIVERED

Most people want their employer to make a profit because everyone knows that unprofitable companies pare their payrolls. But here is a significant question: **Do most of your employees care how much profit your company makes?**

If employees have no stake in the company's relative success—their pay remains essentially constant no matter how the company performs—why should they invest themselves beyond a minimum level?

When your employees' pay isn't tied in some way to the performance of the company, the success of the company becomes incidental to filling the day with minimal keep-from-getting-fired work. An uninspired work force doesn't strive to fulfill the company's potential.

▌ PAY COMMUNICATES

A company that offers no stake in its success to the workers who help create it sends a very negative message to them: We consider you incidental to the organization's success; you are but a necessary tool to executives receiving bonuses.

Workers ask themselves, "Why should I break my back with little possibility of any real reward? I can't get promoted; the company recently eliminated several supervisory layers. And I can't make more than a small increase in pay no matter how hard I work."

▌ CREATED EQUAL, PAID DIFFERENTLY

Most managers instinctively dislike the idea of discriminating between employees when it comes to assessing and rewarding people differently for their performance. So they tend to reward everyone with about the same increase. Apparently, most managers yield to the invisible pull of the American myth that everyone is "created equal." Of course, we don't really believe that everyone is created equal or we'd be living equally under socialism rather than varyingly under capitalism.

If you find yourself confused by competing sympathies on this issue, you're not alone. Our national psyche is torn by competing ethics: equality and meritocracy. We know that some people drive big, expensive cars and live in big, expensive suburban homes, while others can't imagine aspiring to that life. Perhaps if compensation systems were oriented more toward achievement—without dependence on the arbitrary judgment of supervisors who might harbor their own agenda or prejudices—some who now feel shut out from the good life might have a shot at it.

▌ SHARED STAKES, COMMON GOALS

If everyone has a stake in profits or expected outcomes, everyone would be conscious of how they spent the company money directly and indirectly, and how their work might maximize those profits. Teamwork (and peer pressure) would be encouraged. Even people not motivated by acquiring wealth—and there are many—should welcome this arrangement because they want fair compensation relative to what their peers and colleagues receive.

To stimulate better performance without raising compensation costs, quit playing the escalating entitlements game. Make income gains for your workers relative to individual, team, and company performance. For everyone.

R-I-S-K

Gains in compensation should reflect both the company's success and the risk assumed by workers. Risk is a four-letter word which most people find foreign rather than offensive. Stockholders know they risk their financial well-being on company performance, but people inside companies generally do not. Fixed pay may provide some people with a sense of security, though millions of workers in all classes have discovered that it provides no guarantee of employment. Fixed pay doesn't even assure that one can maintain a modest standard of living; workers operating under the flat-pay system actually lost purchasing power in recent years. Even fully salaried employees assume significant risk in their compensation. Their variable is 100 percent, employed or unemployed.

A variable pay program acknowledges risk and provides motivation for better than mediocre performance with the promise of better than mediocre reward.

 ACTION STEPS

☐ Examine your own attitude about pay. Are you willing to put your compensation at risk in exchange for potentially greater rewards than you would otherwise receive?

☐ Determine how willing you are to judge differences

Wilkie

in performance between workers when that means you must pay them at rates that might vary widely. Are you prepared to give substantially greater rewards to your top performers while perhaps giving no increase to your least distinguished employees? Why or why not?

 _____

_____

_____

CHAPTER 5

REMIND PEOPLE OF THEIR HIDDEN COMPENSATION

Benefit costs amount to more than a third of payroll expense. This hidden compensation includes paid days off, medical benefits, unemployment insurance, pensions, and the like. All these goodies come from the same pot of money as the payroll, yet they are invisible to—or at least taken for granted by—most employees. Across the United States, millions of full-time workers have no health insurance while millions of others see it as a free entitlement.

You make a tragic mistake not communicating the true dollar value of the benefits you provide to your workers. If employees quit to strike out on their own, they'd probably be in for a severe shock when trying to replace all the benefits they received at good old Paternal, Inc.

Your corporation spends real dollars that can't be used to pay dividends or increase salaries in order to provide employee benefits of great value. Your employees should understand that and be routinely reminded of it. You also should communicate how those costs have escalated almost exponentially in recent years.

Every paycheck should carry a statement of the value of benefits the employee received during the pay period and year to date.

 ACTION STEPS

☐ Regularly provide employees with a complete

accounting of their *total* compensation and the market value of the benefits they receive.

☐ _____

_____

_____

_____

CHAPTER 6

"BIG MO'" TAKES MORE THAN MONEY

If your employees believe that their work has meaning—that it makes a contribution, that you or someone else appreciates it—then they're motivated. *Motivation* comes from the same root word as "movement." Motivated people are people moved to move. Motivated people are productive. They accomplish extraordinary feats.

How do you get your people to give you their all—their most earnest effort and best thinking? Napoleon Bonaparte said, "There are two levers for moving men: interest and fear."

One lever can move people only to work long and hard. Fear of losing one's job can motivate a person to work overtime and deliver improved productivity for a while, but it is ineffective as a stimulant for innovative enterprise. ("I can't do my best work when I'm distracted by a fear of getting whacked for everything that I do," confides a frazzled manager who works for an unreasonably demanding and vindictive boss.)

The other lever you can pull motivates people both to sweat and think arduously and inventively. Contrasted to fear, interest—a fascination with work that gives employees a psychic investment in it—propels people to undertake whatever is necessary to achieve greatness.

Albert Einstein said that "feeling and desire are the motive forces behind all human endeavor and human creation." Sure, money doesn't hurt either but, like fear, it's not as powerful a motivator as interest and other psychic gratification. **We take fiscal paychecks to the bank every two weeks, but psychic paychecks we take to heart every day.**

█ MORE THAN MONEY

Motivation on the job has far more to do with psychic paychecks than fiscal ones. Look at salespeople. Often they work with no cap on their income. They get paid for the results they produce, usually a result of the effort and creativity they're willing to expend. So sales representatives have a direct monetary incentive: work, produce, receive. Interestingly, companies lavish the most motivational awards, from trophies to trips, on salespeople. Why? Don't salespeople have incentive enough with monetary compensation directly proportional to their achievements? People in sales management understand that while money is important, it doesn't drive people to excel the way psychic compensation does. (Pass the plaques, please.)

💡 ACTION STEPS

☐ Examine what truly motivates you. Assuming reasonably fair compensation, what factors could make the difference between your doing competent work and really giving your all to a project or job?

☐ Honestly evaluate the competitive worth of your organization's fiscal and psychic paychecks. Are they such that employees will be motivated (become excited) to produce great work?

☐ Identify ways you can issue psychic paychecks to

your employees (this book lists quite a few). Resolve
to dispense more of them.

☐ _____

_____

_____

CHAPTER 7

THE MOST POWERFUL MOTIVATOR CAN BE
SUMMED UP IN A SINGLE WORD

Entire books, seminars, audio- and videotapes are devoted to unlocking the mystery of "motivating" employees. While theories and techniques abound, the most profound principle is the simplest. Yet, this intense driver of ambition, commitment, and sacrifice is as elusive as it is effective.

In one word, it explains more than all the books, tapes, and speeches combined. It is a factor of influence without match; a concept that cannot be purchased, manufactured, or falsely employed.

For this most powerful motivator, employees will suffer mediocre wages, poor working conditions, and even physical or mental pain. Some will even give their lives for it.

The most powerful motivator is simply *purpose*.

HOW PURPOSE MOTIVATES

Infused with purpose, teachers of modest means dip into their own pockets to buy materials for their classes when their employer won't. Sustained by purpose, a secretary cheerfully stays in the same poorly paying job for an entire career. Gripped by purpose, police officers and other brave souls risk their lives for comparatively paltry compensation. Filled with purpose, volunteers give of their time and talents; volunteer firefighters will even put their lives on the line for nothing more than a chance to help their neighbors. Possessed by purpose, people will give of themselves in a manner that no employer could rightfully ask or direct.

Purpose provides rewards beyond mere monetary compensation in the currency of involvement, fulfillment, and contribution to something *important.* This is central to what makes every one of us tick. Purpose fulfills the need to be needed.

Inspired work comes from passion borne of purpose.

💡 ACTION STEPS

☐ Help your employees to understand the *effect* of their work: the joy or help others receive from their output.

☐ Instill a sense of pride in your organization. Remind your employees of the contributions the organization—and their work—makes to your customers, community, and charities.

☐ Exemplify a sense of purpose in your work. Keep sarcasm and cynicism at bay. Enthusiasm for your work will become irresistibly contagious to those around you.

☐ Nurture your own sense of purpose in your work. If you feel it waning, rediscover the thrill you experienced when you first entered your line of work. If it was exciting then, it can be exciting now even though things may have changed. If you can't touch that part of you that once burst with joy in your work, consider a change of employer or career.

☐ _____

_____

_____

CHAPTER 8

THE PHYSIOLOGY OF WORK PSYCHOLOGY

Motivated people are *physiologically* different from apathetic or depressed workers. If you've ever attended an inspiring seminar or stimulating meeting, or engaged in work personally meaningful, you know that "fired-up" feeling. It's more than a mental state. The pulse quickens, the adrenaline flows, and the sparked imagination releases the brain's endorphins and ignites the neural connectors in rapid fire. Your heart is pounding, your mind is racing. You're poised to perform at your peak.

Exciting work makes us high.

As a manager, you can take advantage of the way nature creates a physical response to psychological involvement in work. Use this self-reinforcing phenomenon to **create a work environment for your employees that is literally stimulating.**

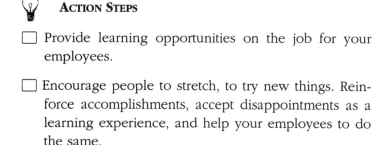 **ACTION STEPS**

☐ Provide learning opportunities on the job for your employees.

☐ Encourage people to stretch, to try new things. Reinforce accomplishments, accept disappointments as a learning experience, and help your employees to do the same.

☐ Keep a sense of urgency and importance to the work

your group does. Keep progress against goals top
of mind for everyone: Publish deadlines, post results.

☐ _____

_____

_____

CHAPTER 9

CREATE AN EXCLUSIVE MEMBERSHIP

Picture Edison, Marconi, and other renowned inventors toiling away to make the big breakthrough. Did you imagine them working in virtually solitary confinement? In our technologically advanced world, innovation is not restricted to the inventor's bench or lab, and it's not a solo sport. Innovation frequently comes from teamwork performed in large companies.

Your organization, or your corner of it, can incubate creativity rather than stifle it, even if you invent nothing more than ways to pinch pennies. The organization provides physical and technical resources, as well as social and psychic support, which can help spur innovators to greatness.

Creatively productive teamwork can be enhanced by creating a sense of belonging to an exclusive club. *This* is the place to be. Great work is done here. The ad agency for the U.S. Marine Corps knew the powerful attraction of pride in belonging when it created the recruiting slogan, "The few. The proud. The Marines."

At one of my employers, people in my group proudly called themselves *The A-Team*. I didn't assign the label to our group, but I saw how it gave the team an identity as one that produces more work better and faster than any other in the industry.

Justifiable boasting is a great motivator. It ties performance to pride in one's superior work, faith in co-workers, and satisfaction with one's employer.

ACTION STEPS

☐ Signal your own pleasure with and faith in your employer.

☐ Hold your group's best work—or your plan for it— up against that of competing organizations. Proudly point out the superiority of your employees' work product. If the comparison is unfavorable, thoroughly plan an attack on the common enemy: mediocrity. Express confidence in your group's ability to best the current standard. Pledge your commitment to attaining that goal. Monitor progress, insisting that only great work is acceptable. Recognize progress. Celebrate success, reminding everyone that it resulted from an extraordinary group working together to bring about extraordinary achievements.

☐ _____

   _____

   _____

CHAPTER 10

PUBLICLY CONFER APPRECIATION

Two forces converge in today's corporations to make recognition for performance much more potent and necessary. First, organizations are eliminating middle management jobs by the millions, resulting in fewer opportunities for people to receive promotions. Second, this trend comes just as the great swell of baby boomers reaches the age when they expected to move up the ladder. Baby boomers and their younger—and equally frustrated—peers need affirmations outside ascendancy in the ranks.

UNNOTICED AND UNDERVALUED

Most engineers, financial analysts, warehouse supervisors, scientists, secretaries, computer programmers, lawyers, trainers, production workers and middle managers toil in obscurity. Their valuable contributions are invisible and under-appreciated.

While the pride of authorship is mitigated by the anonymity of most people's labor, recognition by one's bosses (or peers) offers some consolation. It validates hard work. It says, *we care as much about your work as you do.*

Recognizing good performance doesn't just mean verbal pats on the back. Shouting "good job, good job" with abandon cheapens praise just as printing too much money devalues currency. The point is to pay people something extra, something not compensable by any merit increase.

THE MAGIC OF CEREMONY

Since human beings first sat around a campfire, they have engaged in ceremonial rituals paying tribute to the best in the tribe. Extending recognition to deserving and unsung heroes in the modern organization is easy with simple awards such as plaques and certificates (and much less sooty than a campfire). A variation on the public acclaim theme is to arrange for publicity in a company, industry, or community publication. Public recognition gives an achiever-in-waiting outward affirmation that he or she is an important member of the company's society.

Some solemn business people believe that recognition awards are silly. "People who win awards don't think that," chuckles Dave Tanner, a soft-spoken, serious man with a Ph.D. in polymer science. As an executive with DuPont, Tanner used awards to encourage practical and profitable innovations by his technical staff in the industrial fibers division. Fond of Rodin's *The Thinker,* Tanner gave out the statue in "all different sizes" as awards for Creative Thinking, Creative Leadership, and other categories of successful ideas. Some came with checks, some didn't. Tanner believes such awards motivate all their acclaimed recipients.

In addition to the motivating effect of saying "thank you," awards telegraph to the whole staff: *This is what we mean by good work here.* And there is yet another value to public recognition. "Publicly confer on people a high expectation and they will keep rising to fulfill it," says a senior executive friend of mine. He calls business achievement awards Wizard of Oz motivation. "You have a brain because this piece of paper certifies that you do."

When you have the good fortune to have some consistently solid performers, you might feel uncomfortable fre-

"Gosh, I didn't think anybody noticed that my new accounting method saved us a billion last year!"

quently saluting them in public or plying them with plaques. A way to say thanks to them is to mark their birthdays or their company anniversaries with a personal note in a card and some modest ceremonial gift. I once received an unexpected bottle of bubbly on the anniversary of my start date and it made me feel wonderful.

💡 ACTION STEPS

☐ List public recognition opportunities available in your organization.

☐ Assess how well you take advantage of those opportunities. Commit to using them, or creating occasions and methods for recognizing great work.

☐ _____

_____

_____

CHAPTER 11

SAY THANK YOU WITH A GESTURE

A great commercial for American Airlines shows a tired businessman returning in the night to his darkened office to see the answering machine light blinking. The exhausted exec drops into a chair and hits play to hear a message to this effect, "Well done, Jack. There's a little something for you in your top drawer." Jack opens the drawer and pulls out some American Airlines tickets. A smile comes to his reinvigorated face. Jack is ready to take on the world once again.

Thank you gestures need not be that lavish. As the saying goes, it's the thought that counts. Say thank you with a funny card, flowers, plants, or a favorite snack or beverage left with a handwritten note on the desk or in the work area. How about lottery tickets ("While you're on such a hot streak . . ." or "I'm lucky that you work here."), tickets to a play or the movies, or a gift certificate for a store or restaurant?

Reward with prizes that help encourage even better performance: books, audio- or videotapes, or a magazine subscription. Information in America is mass marketed at ridiculously low cost (the price of books, for example) and can yield benefits exponential to the negligible investment.

Some companies have policies against paying for such "gifts" to employees (mine does though I would prefer the company to provide the money out of the compensation budget). Managers who recognize the power of recognition often reward employees out of their own pockets. They understand that they are investing in their own success by investing in the people who work for them.

💡 **ACTION STEPS**

☐ Appreciate people's need to be appreciated.

☐ Use tangible items, carefully selected to reflect an individual's preferences, to signal your gratitude for extraordinary accomplishment.

☐ Encourage your organization to adopt a "spot bonus" policy that will provide at least a modest budget to pay for inexpensive recognition items. The power is in the symbolism, not the value of the gift.

☐ _____

_____

_____

CHAPTER 12

CORRECT WITH PRIDE

Recognize the conundrum you create when you bolster your employees' ego involvement in their work. By recognizing people for jobs well done, you encourage them to assume personal responsibility for what they produce. You also create a condition where it's difficult for employees not to take work-related criticism personally.

How do you criticize and correct without offending? The value-adding manager does it with care, objective information, and a solid vote of confidence in superior performance in the future.

ACTION STEPS

☐ Bring unacceptable work immediately to the attention of those responsible.

☐ In a calm, even tone of voice, explain why the work is not up to standard and the consequences of the poor quality.

☐ Ask, with no implied threat, what factors contributed to delivering undesirable results.

☐ Make clear that you expect not perfection but consistent quality, and that you accept the reality that even the most attentive and considerate person can make mistakes.

☐ In a caring tone, ask for recommendations that would prevent this from happening again.

31

☐ Thank the employees for their candor and help.

☐ Express your appreciation for the usually excellent work produced by the employees who erred, and your confidence in their capabilities to produce outstanding work on a continual basis.

☐ _____

_____

_____

CHAPTER 13

BE A GENIUS

In Roman mythology, a "genius" was a spirit that guided a person. Individuals who accomplished something often attributed their success to this genius. As a value-adding manager, you must be like a genius to your employees, inspiring (which means to breathe life into) great accomplishments.

You already know that recognition, fair pay, and incentives help to spur productivity. Here's a profound truth you may not have thought about: **The most powerful motivator for ingenious work is *meaningful* work.** When people believe they are participating in work that is *important*, it gives rise to *enthusiasm* which literally means "to be inspired by a god."

ACTION STEPS

☐ Explain to your employees how their work contributes to the mission of the organization. Give them the big picture and illustrate how their own work fits into the whole.

☐ Report frequently on the progress of the organization in relation to its goals. Help your employees to see that their individual efforts matter and are part of something worth working for.

☐ _____

_____

_____

CHAPTER 14

COMMUNICATE FACE TO FACE

A big part of positively influencing behavior is direct personal communication. Issuing memos or distributing information released by Human Resources doesn't constitute communicating.

EXPLAIN HOW TASKS MAKE A CONTRIBUTION

When you delegate assignments to people, tell them about the larger implications of their actions. That "bigger picture" perspective will help people to understand how their actions effect a solution. It gives them a psychic investment in their work; nothing motivates good performance more than appreciating how important one's work is.

SLEEP ON YOUR MEMOS

While face-to-face communication is nearly always preferable to written communication, when you need to communicate strongly worded messages, write down your thoughts first. That will help you focus clearly on the important issues. Then put the memo in a "24-hour drawer." Do the same with electronic mail. Delay your impulse to send an immediate response to an inflammatory or aggravating message.

No one likes to be on the receiving end of a "flamer," but they can really knock sensitive employees off-kilter for days, weeks, maybe evermore. If what you wrote today has merit, it still will tomorrow. Angry, self-righteous memos have a way of sounding pretty stupid after a night's sleep. If, in the new day's dawn, you feel comfortable with what you wrote yesterday, send it. If not, destroy it or start over.

GET OUT AND INTERACT

Throw away your out basket. By delivering memos to your staff in person, you'll increase the chance of informal conversation about things they're working on. Those chats can yield good information and insights. Ideas spring from informal exchanges as often—or more so—as from formal meetings.

LISTEN TO COMMUNICATE

A value-adding manager understands that communicating doesn't mean talking. Sending messages is far less than half the communication equation. Messages sent have meaning only in the minds of the receiver. What you meant to mean means nothing if it isn't the meaning in the minds of those who (mis)receive your message. (Go ahead, read that again!)

The real action in communication for the value-adding manager is in listening. We'll never know more than we know now unless we open our minds to new knowledge.

WATCH YOUR MOUTH

The value-adding manager recognizes the importance of language as an agent of influence in the workplace. Each conversation with a colleague, especially one who reports to you, is similar to a financial transaction. Communication exchanges are hardly ever neutral; they register as positive or negative.

One of the most overwhelmingly powerful positive communication transactions takes no more than two words. People will walk barefoot on a bed of hot coals for you if they believe you'll appreciate it. Take a second a few times each day to say "Thank you."

▍ No Buts

An overlooked but powerful negative communicator is the phrase "yes, but." While you may be saying yes to show you understand, when you say that little word *but* you've wiped out everything that preceded it in the mind of the listener. "I think you're a nice person, *but* . . ." See?

▍ Ask

When you need to bring your experience to bear in directing a project's progress, instead of issuing orders, try asking questions. **What would happen if we approached it this way?** Questions stimulate thinking. They might point one in a certain direction, but they're still open-ended allowing for the contribution of some additional generative thinking.

 Action Steps

☐ Tell people why their work is important.

☐ Dump your out basket. Deliver communications in person.

☐ Wait a day before sending any negative communication.

☐ Listen.

☐ Chose your words carefully.

☐ Lead by questioning.

☐ _____
_____
_____

CHAPTER 15

Do As You Say You'd Do

As a manager, you are a role model. By simple virtue of your position, your influence extends wide and far. This role falls to you even if you'd rather not accept it. It is conferred, not taken.

The value-adding manager models the kind of employee he or she wants to work with. Inconsistency in word and deed—hypocrisy—demoralizes employees, especially those sensitive people who often have the most to give. I've worked with executives who have spent hours anguishing over every word of the text for a routine "pinch-every-penny-for-austerity" speech to employees (of which no one remembers a single word five minutes after the presentation), but no time thinking about how their flagrantly lavish lunches communicated a contrary message much more clearly.

COMPENSATORY MANAGEMENT DIRECTIVES

Deeds not mirroring words are often evidenced by the "compensatory management directive." Sometimes managers admit weaknesses only in their subconscious while apologizing for their true nature. (This principle can be seen in all walks of life. Alfred Nobel, the fellow who established the Nobel Peace Prize, was the son of a land- and naval-mine inventor, and Alfred, too, invented explosives including dynamite.)

A few examples of the "compensatory management directive." An executive I once worked with had no appreciable people skills; he was short of temper, secretive, mercurial, frequently offensive in his language, and flip-flopped decisions without telling most of those affected. The kicker: He often gave to his staff articles and books on communication and people management!

Another manager I worked with trusted *no one*: he forbade contact with employees outside his department, insisted on reviewing all internal memoranda before distribution, was highly secretive about the most mundane things, and pumped people for office gossip. He insisted that his whole staff—except himself, of course—attend elaborate "teamwork" workshops.

A trade association executive told me about a board member who insisted that the professional staff attend creativity workshops to infuse some innovative thinking into the organization. Learning their lessons well, the staff came back to the office bursting with new ideas—none of which were implemented. Seems that a certain board member really wasn't too fond of change.

Perhaps these executives believed that the purity of their occasional good intentions compensated for their otherwise overbearing behavior. However, the intensity of one's preaching cannot overcome the repugnance of one's actions.

WORDS VERSUS DEEDS

There is no contest between your words and deeds. A Japanese proverb holds that "sooner or later you act out what you really think." A modern management axiom suggests that you "walk the walk before you talk the talk."

Your employees learn far more by watching you in action than listening to anything you say. Save your breath; speak in bold body language that inspires imitation.

ACTION STEPS

☐ Ask yourself, "Are my words and deeds consistent?" Ask your staff and your boss the same question.

☐ Imagine a camera crew constantly following you around at work, recording your every move. Would you want your boss and staff to see that tape? Would you want your employees imitating the star of that tape?

☐ Eliminate actions and habits that are inconsistent with the way a good manager should behave. Act like the manager you'd want to work for.

☐ _____

_____

_____

CHAPTER 16

COMPLIMENT WITH YOUR UNDIVIDED ATTENTION

Your personal attention to someone can be rewarding by itself. As organizations streamline, more managers are player/coaches personally performing tasks that in cushier times they would have delegated to others, or they are now supervising more people—affording less time for personal contact with each, or both. Advanced electronic communication also greatly minimizes the need for human contact to exchange information. In my office, the local area network on my personal computer and the voice mail on my phone allow me to communicate instantly with everyone in the company without ever leaving my chair.

The technology leads to more autonomy for my colleagues, which might be liberating but just as likely is alienating. We inhabit the same space but often communicate as though we were separated by thousands of miles, receiving information without benefit of the nuances of personal contact. Passing along information by machine denies people valuable feedback on whether they're doing what the company expects. The isolation demotivates.

Value-adding managers take time for the people who report to them and make a point to visit with them. I think of intentional face-to-face communication with employees as "watering." It's refreshing and sustaining for everyone. While watering won't guarantee that employees will blossom, it's a pretty good hedge against their withering.

Take the time to *listen*. Listening is so powerful a motivator that many people are treated for their psychological needs by professionals who do little more than hear them out. Letting someone blow off steam helps them relieve the mental pressure that can build so quickly in our fast-paced, understaffed organizations.

A complimentary way of spending time with an employee is to share some appropriate, confidential information. It acknowledges the person's judgment. So does asking, "What do you think of the way we're doing things?" Ask for advice about some challenge you face in your responsibilities. You'll get a fresh perspective and maybe some new ideas that you can really use and wouldn't otherwise have.

⌾ ACTION STEPS

☐ Make a point of visiting with the people who report to you. Schedule the interactions so that they really take place.

☐ Stimulate interaction by asking thought-provoking questions instead of pontificating. Find out what's working and what's not.

☐ Take notes.

☐ Take action on problems or opportunities raised in the conversation.

☐ Schedule your next visit.

☐ _____

_____

_____

Chapter 17

Don't Expect HR to Train Your Employees

Training shouldn't be left to the Human Resources Department or mistaken for learning. Dave Tanner, a former DuPont executive, says **one trains animals but educates people.** Educating employees to help them fulfill their potential means focusing on more than job functions.

As a value-adding manager, you are an educator. That doesn't mean simply expounding your own knowledge but finding educational opportunities for the people who report to you. One of the ways I've done that in my own shop is occasionally to make staff meetings a partial learning session. I invite people from other parts of the company to come explain what they do even if it has no direct bearing on my group. The more employees know about the *business*, the better they understand the context of their work and the more contribution they can make to it.

ACTION STEPS

☐ Take personal responsibility for providing education for the people who report to you.

☐ Specify the skills and knowledge you'd like your staff to acquire.

☐ Identify opportunities to provide the missing skills or enhance existing ones.

☐ Give people time off to go to the library, to visit with

friends at other organizations to observe their methods, or to read a skill-enhancing book at home for a day or two.

☐ _____

_____

_____

CHAPTER 18

SPECIFY GOALS NOT METHODS

You can easily burn more time than you can afford trying to determine both what needs to be done and how to get it done. Value-adding managers encourage their people to reach goals and solve problems using innovative methods of their own design.

Your job is to set the agenda and monitor results. Your staff's job is to create activities that produce the results to the standards you set.

The value-adding manager specifies objectives, not methods.

ACTION STEPS

☐ Review your interactions with your employees (conversations, memos, E-mail messages). Are you telling them how to accomplish tasks as well as indicating what needs to be done?

☐ Let go of the belief that "my way is the best way." Your employees can help you most when they learn—sometimes by making mistakes—how to create solutions to challenges on their own.

☐ Rather than telling your employees how to do a task, ask them how they plan to do it. Give them an opportunity to think about the challenge, to develop alternatives, and to implement the methods they believe will work best.

☐ _____

_____

_____

CHAPTER 19

QUALITY IS A LEARNING EXPERIENCE

There is no room for second rate in today's competitive climate. You must set high standards and hold people accountable for maintaining them. But beware the perfection infection (see Chapter 42). You can't nitpick great performance out of anyone.

Define what you mean by high-quality work. If you can't write down a specification, publicly point to it whenever you see it both inside your organization and outside it. A value-adding manager is keeper of the flame of quality for him- or herself and the work unit; he or she helps everyone to understand that maintaining high standards can be a learning event.

If things aren't up to standard, ask your colleagues to investigate. They should ask: Why did we fail to deliver good work? What should be done differently? What are all the possible consequences of changing a process, supplier, deadline, etc.?

By taking ownership of this learning process, your employees will acquire knowledge that will help them to improve the business, not just fix the broken expectation. And quality will not simply be maintained, but increase.

ACTION STEPS

☐ Define what you mean by high-quality work.

☐ View subpar performance as an occasion for learning.

☐ Instruct your employees to determine why unaccept-able work was delivered and to create systems or procedures to prevent a recurrence. Ask them to use their new knowledge to improve the business.

☐ _____
_____
_____

CHAPTER 20

HOLD PRODUCTIVE MEETINGS

Meetings should be used for exchanging information interactively with your staff, not as a forum for you to dispense information. When several people contribute to a meeting, there's an opportunity for everyone to draw on the cumulative decades of life experience in the room. When the boss does all the talking, there's a limited base of information and experience no matter how impressive.

One way to put people's minds in a receptive mood for exchanging information is to open routine meetings by asking, "What have you read, seen or heard in the last week that made an impression on you?" The purpose of the question is not to stir up an off-point gabfest, but to get each attendee to make an initial verbal contribution and to expand everyone's mental frame of reference. This brief exercise will make for better thinking in the meeting when you quickly return to the prepared agenda.

Always close your meetings with a review of the decisions so that there are no misunderstandings. Also review all pending action items, making clear who will undertake them. Then reiterate the deadlines; projects without deadlines amount to nothing more than a wish list.

HOLD THE ANCHOVIES

For the price of a few pizzas and sodas, a lunch meeting can contribute a great deal of insight into the business. I usually avoid food at meetings (they aren't parties) but sometimes a few pizzas on the table make for a better meeting.

"Everybody has a vastly greater potential for creative and innovative thinking than the routine workday allows," says Mark Sebell, formerly with Colgate-Palmolive and now a principal with Creative Realities. Pizza—and the casual conversation that inevitably accompanies it—seems just enough out of the routine to help people relax and make contributions they might otherwise not.

ACTION STEPS

☐ Get all your staff talking at meetings.

☐ Close meetings by reviewing who is going to do what, and the deadlines for all actions.

☐ Use pizza and soda on occasion to break up the monotony of the staff meeting ritual. Let the conversation flow and watch it lead to some great insights you wouldn't otherwise have reached.

☐ _____

_____

_____

CHAPTER 21

SEEK GREAT THINKING FROM YOUR EMPLOYEES

To be an effective boss, you need not be a power station of new ideas, just a lightning rod for them. Reject the old prejudice that only some people are creative. "Naturally" creative people like entrepreneurs and artists may simply possess an innate ability to freely express their creativity; others may only need permission to use theirs. Once I gave a speech in New York City on "Where Do Ideas Come From?" In the speech, I suggested several techniques by which one might generate more ideas. I urged the business audience to think of creativity as a set of learned skills and behaviors. Following the speech, an old-line industrialist in the audience rose to take me to task for the *faulty premise* I advanced. "Most people aren't creative. Those that are become the bosses, the artists, but everyone else, well they just don't have it," he scolded.

ASK—AND RESPOND—TO RECEIVE

The value-adding manager knows that *all* people are capable of suggesting better ideas. Often, it only takes a sincere invitation ("I need your help with some ideas for . . .") to get helpful ideas flowing.

Value-adding managers affirm their commitment to everyone making a creative contribution to the business by welcoming suggestions and then *responding* to the ideas they receive. An idea has no value if no one does anything with it; and people aren't encouraged to come up with a new batch of ideas when they don't know what happened to the last batch. Take every staff idea seriously and consider each one fully.

SAY "NO" AFFIRMATIVELY

If you do a good job creating an atmosphere that invites creative contributions from your staff, you'll find yourself saying *no* more often. Chances are many ideas simply won't be appropriate for immediate implementation. And even in the "keeper" pile, there'll be some you need to reject because you won't have the resources to implement every good idea you receive.

Say no with compassion; denying someone's idea is a little like murder in that you kill a part of the employee's psychic investment that went into formulating and proposing that concept. An effective way to take the sting out of rejecting an idea is to explain why the suggestion is not appropriate *at this time*, and to promise at the same time to keep the idea on file for future reference when changing conditions may make the idea perfectly applicable.

With the broader context your explanation provides, the person who submitted the idea may go back and reframe the concept to fit more appropriately, or begin a whole new, and more productive, line of thinking.

FRESH IDEAS FROM FRESH EYES

Another great way to get new ideas about how your internal operation is running is to use the fresh insights of newly hired employees. Ask them to observe your operation and make notes about what doesn't make sense to

them. About four or five weeks into their tenure, ask them to provide you with their observations in writing. Then encourage them to keep making notes for another brief report in about six months.

To keep a stream of good ideas constantly flowing, be accessible and responsive. React to employees' ideas before you forget about them. Or your enthusiastic staff implements them.

 ACTION STEPS

☐ Ask your employees, including new hires, to come up with some ideas to help you solve problems or create opportunities.

☐ When someone submits an idea to you, thank the person for contributing, and promise to fully consider the idea and report back within 48 hours on the prospects for implementing the proposal.

☐ If you need more information to fully consider the suggestion, ask the employee who submitted the idea to do the homework.

☐ If you can't use the idea that your employee proposed, explain why. Promise to keep the suggestion on file, and make a commitment to review the idea periodically because changing circumstances may suddenly make the idea applicable.

☐ Review, every quarter or at least every six months, those suggestions that you rejected earlier. Examine whether a proposed idea or variation on the theme might now make more sense than when you first received the proposal.

☐ After implementing an idea proposed by an employee, publicly acknowledge (at a meeting, in a newsletter or memo) the employee's important contribution. Encourage others to make their contributions.

☐ _____

_____

_____

CHAPTER 22

ENCOURAGE ACHIEVEMENT

Anyone who has ever participated in sporting events or witnessed them firsthand knows the power of affirmation. What is the "hometown advantage" but simply the power of lots of positive feedback. Value-adding managers don't carry pompoms, do cartwheels, and shout "good job, good job." Rather, they quietly affirm. Cheerleading works not because it's flashy or noisy, but because it affects people powerfully. It makes people feel better and, because they do, perform better.

Cheerleading can take many forms: psychic incentives, compensation, and affirming organizational policies. Among the most effective is treating people like capable adults. If your employees believe they have your trust and confidence, they'll work hard to keep it. People's estimates of their own abilities are often tied to your estimates of them. One of the most powerful motivational speeches on earth is only six words long: "I believe you can do it."

 ACTION STEPS

☐ Recognize good performance by your staff; let your employees know you notice and appreciate good work.

☐ Instill confidence in your employees by assigning them high standards to maintain, and communicate

your faith in their ability to meet and exceed those
standards.

☐ _____

_____

_____

CHAPTER 23

REWARD WITH PERSONAL GROWTH

Turn a good performance into a better one by rewarding someone with an opportunity to develop even more skills.

ACTION STEPS

☐ Send the top performer to a conference or course of his or her choosing.

☐ Arrange a trip to a company operation in or near a desirable destination. Exposing key people to more insight on how the company operates serves everyone; the desirable locale affords a little mix of business and pleasure.

☐ Make a point to provide opportunities for the newly educated to use the new knowledge on the job.

☐ _____
_____
_____

CHAPTER 24

A MORALE PROBLEM IS A MANAGEMENT PROBLEM

A monk joins a monastery where he must take a vow of silence. He is allowed to say only two words every decade. The monk's daily routine consists of rising from a bed that's no more than a plank at 3:30 A.M., praying while kneeling for hours on a stone floor, eating tasteless gruel, and copying Bibles by hand. The monk follows this routine day after day after long day for 10 straight years without uttering a word. One day the abbot summons the monk and grants him permission to say his allotted two words. The monk looks up at the abbot with tired eyes and says, "Bed hard." Having said this, the monk returns to his daily grind of rising at 3:30 A.M., praying, eating tasteless gruel, copying Bibles by hand, and sleeping on a bed that's no more than a plank. Another year goes by. Then another. Then five. Then 10. After 20 years of this unvarying routine, the monk is again summoned to appear before the abbot who permits him to speak two words. Without hesitation, the monk snorts, "Food lousy," and returns to his dreary routine. After another silent decade of pre-dawn awakenings, tasteless gruel, arduous copying, painful prayer and restless sleep on a plank, the monk again reports to the abbot to speak his two words. The bent, tired and frail monk looks up at the abbot and says, "I quit." The abbot snaps back, "Fine! You've done nothing but complain since the moment you got here."

Lackluster employee motivation is the leading gripe of

managers pressured to produce results. That's a serious problem because we're asking our employees to do more work to higher standards in less time and with fewer resources. Those are pretty tall orders for people who have no major stake in the incremental success of the business.

Isn't it ironic that bosses who place such importance on motivation are often the same ones who reject simple programs to enrich worker satisfaction, terming them "soft" and "unbusinesslike." If workers' enthusiasm for their jobs weren't truly important, no one would ever need to talk about a morale problem.

To help combat sagging morale, companies collectively spend millions on motivational minstrels who, if they're good enough, help employees find renewed excitement for their jobs—for about an hour or until they go back to work. The value-adding manager knows that **motivation problems aren't fixed by pep rallies.** I've accepted speaking engagements to address employees whose boss described them as suffering from a lack of motivation. Invariably, at the end of the presentation—usually in the hotel lobby or company parking lot—I'd get questions like "How do we get the boss to stop being such an s.o.b.," or to "do what needs to be done to save the business?"

RECIPROCAL MOTIVATION

The Law of Reciprocal Motivation states: Employee morale mirrors management's commitment. If you notice that your employees' motivation level isn't as high as it should be, you're actually perceiving worker frustration. Employees who complain are usually bewildered by an organization that doesn't value their contribution or inhibits them from working to their capacity. Almost everyone desperately wants to do good work. So many times I've heard employees say, "How we're doing this makes no sense! It's not efficient. We tell management and they don't do anything about it." In circumstances like that, people give up hope and hold back their best ideas and energy. I call this condition the Reciprocal Motivation Deficit: "If you don't care, then I don't care."

Morale problems aren't symptomatic of problems in the workforce. They do, however, speak volumes about management.

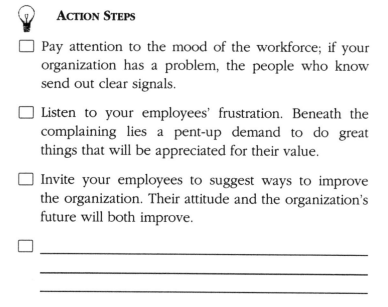

ACTION STEPS

☐ Pay attention to the mood of the workforce; if your organization has a problem, the people who know send out clear signals.

☐ Listen to your employees' frustration. Beneath the complaining lies a pent-up demand to do great things that will be appreciated for their value.

☐ Invite your employees to suggest ways to improve the organization. Their attitude and the organization's future will both improve.

☐ _____

   _____

   _____

CHAPTER 25

QUESTION RULES AND PROCEDURES

Bureaucracy is the natural enemy of greatness. Unnecessary procedures, outdated rules, and other senselessly self-imposed strictures smother innovation. **People can't do their best work when they're fighting a system that prevents them from doing it.**

💡 **ACTION STEPS**

☐ Constantly evaluate your firm's (and your own) policies and methods. Ask yourself and your employees:
   ☐ What are we doing?
   ☐ Why are we doing it?
   ☐ Does it need to be done?
   ☐ What are better ways to do it?

☐ Invite everyone working for you to nominate restrictive or useless policies for elimination.

☐ When you've uncovered some time-wasters, hold a public execution. With some celebration and ceremony, tear up or burn useless forms or pages from policy manuals that no longer govern make-work activity.

☐ Post signs advising, "Assume nothing. Challenge everything." Or, "Why?"

☐ _____
_____

CHAPTER 26

BAN DEPARTMENTS

The literal meaning of the term *department* is "to divide"—not a useful function when you're trying to compete (literally, "strive together"). The word *department* sounds like *compartment,* and people have far too long treated their departments as self-contained compartments.

Eliminate *department* from your vocabulary and substitute the term *work team*: It implies a task-focused unit of cooperative individuals rather than a fiefdom unto itself. Another advantage to the work team is that individuals in them can change with the tasks. Departments are rigid, prescribed, and insular; work teams are flexible, adaptive, and open.

Members of work teams have a primary assignment in identifiable functional areas (production, promotion, accounting) but might serve on several task-oriented work teams. The work team concept functions best when its members are drawn from across the organization, so members of a given team might represent functional areas such as marketing, MIS, research, manufacturing, and so on.

Explain to your people that task-driven work teams tend to be temporary and less rigid in hierarchy than the old, rock-solid departmental structure. Working in such a fluid environment often requires a greater tolerance for ambiguity, a greater need to participate actively in meetings, and a greater need to follow up with peers across the old organizational lines to ensure that tasks are on track.

ACTION STEPS

☐ Eliminate *department* from your vocabulary and substitute the term *work team.*

☐ Encourage your employees to think of the tasks that need to be accomplished as primary, not the organizational structure around them.

☐ _____

_____

_____

CHAPTER 27

TEAR DOWN MENTAL ELECTRIC FENCES

When I was 12 years old, my family moved from the inner city to the country. As I began to explore the new environment, I was amazed at how dairy cows knew where one farmer's property ended and another's began. With nothing more restrictive than widely spaced fence posts, the cows seemed happily contained on their owner's land. One day, filled with curiosity and the courage to trespass, I decided to take a closer look. As I went deeper into the grassland, I noticed that there was a kind of fence ringing the field. But it surely wasn't substantial; heck, it was nothing but an itty-bitty filament. Why, a cow that must weigh at least a thousand pounds could surely trample this little line with no effort at all!

I reckoned that a closer look was in order. Filled with that curiosity and courage, I set out to test the strength of that tiny cable. I stepped back a few feet and ran at that puny fence. My charge was abruptly short-circuited by a charge of a different sort. Zap! My momentum knocked down the nearest fence post and the brief encounter with the wire knocked me on my fanny. The powerful punch of that thin, nearly invisible wire made a lasting impression on me. And it provides us with a metaphor for a serious issue in managing people.

Cows learn to suppress their innate wanderlust after one or two highly charged encounters with the small but powerful line. In the same way, people—highly intelligent entities with judgment and free will—learn to restrain their innate urges to create at the workplace following one or two zaps by a boss, a creature whose small frame belies his awesome power over others. Employees build their own fences around the urge to share their creative ideas with corporate higher-ups, lest they risk a more powerful, even deadly, shock from the boss. People, even self-assured highfliers, learn to constrain themselves (by matters of degree!), causing internal tension for them and lost opportunities for their employers.

When you finish this book you may charge into the office to announce with great and earnest enthusiasm, "Okay everybody, I want your ideas!" You'll likely be met with dull stares, a few cynical snickers, and some muttering of obscenities. Expect to wait a long time for the floodgates to open.

THE TRUST BARRIER

Survey after survey shows that about 60 percent (or more) of employees at almost all levels don't trust their bosses. Little wonder managers aren't overrun with productive suggestions from their reports.

If most people, even large numbers in the management ranks, don't believe the organization allows for free expression of thought, ideas won't seep naturally into the innovation pipeline and they may not make it there even if management tries to channel them. The walls seem impenetrable.

So how do you effectively release and direct the productive creative energies of system-bucking mavericks and the larger group of achievers-in-waiting? How do you tear down their mental electric fences? Much of this book strives to answer that question.

"It translates — 'but we've always done it
this way - why change?'."

To Catch Some Monkeys

When zookeepers need to catch monkeys for their exhibits, they don't need to chase or lasso them. Monkey hunters place plastic bottles filled with nuts on the ground. As the hunters watch from the bush, hungry monkeys scamper to the bottles with the treasure inside and slip their hands down the bottles' necks. As they try to retrieve their prize, the monkeys discover they're the victims of a clever trick: The bottle necks aren't wide enough to withdraw a clenched fist chock-full of nuts. Greed keeps the monkeys from releasing their bounty; the bottle-manacle prevents them from escaping the monkey hunter's net.

Managers with a tight-fisted grip around their organization's control resemble the self-imprisoned monkeys; they are held captive by their fears. A boss who does not trust his or her people cannot expect their trust in return. To free our hands from the control bottle, to remove the electric fences from the heads of our employees, we must trust and be trustworthy. We must send our co-workers a clear signal that they have permission to contribute their unique insights and talents to the company's challenges, even if it means questioning time-honored traditions.

ACTION STEPS

☐ Recognize the reality that many employees come into your employment distrusting management.

☐ Take heart that you can build trust, and accept the fact that the process takes much longer than you probably want.

☐ To build trust, show your own vulnerabilities. Admit mistakes. Tell tales of blunders (earlier in your career, of course) that taught you valuable lessons.

☐ Most important, to build trust from those you want to trust you, trust them. Visibly.

☐ _____

_____

_____

CHAPTER 28

PUSH THE STANDARDS

If you raise your work standards reasonably, people will aspire to meet them. Expecting better work from people prevents the work atmosphere from becoming stale with predictability. More importantly, it encourages continually better work which yields a reinforcing sense of accomplishment.

A little intramural competition can also raise standards and productivity. Advertising agencies typically pit internal teams against one another to provoke more and better creativity. Motorola sponsors intracompany competition as an exercise to build esprit de corps among corporate staff teams around the world. The participants work on three- to six-month projects related to the company's key goals. They are judged on their competence in the use of analytic tools and teamwork in arriving at solutions, and the effectiveness of their efforts. The company sponsors the competition to emphasize employee participation in solving problems, recognize outstanding performance, encourage continuous improvement, demonstrate the power of teamwork, and recognize top team achievements.

Push your vendors to raise their standards. It's hard to be better than your weakest component. Motorola, a Malcolm Baldrige Quality Award winner, insists that its suppliers apply for the prize.

 ACTION STEPS

☐ Communicate clearly to your employees what you expect from their work, specifying high standards.

Often people don't produce what their boss wants because the expectations weren't clear.

☐ Provide education so your staff can achieve the goals. People can't produce what they're not capable of producing.

☐ Insist that your crew meet the goals. Monitor their progress and offer help along the way.

☐ Reward everyone for achieving the objectives (fiscal and psychic paychecks).

☐ Raise the standards again. That's how you stay on top of the game.

☐ _____

_____

_____

CHAPTER 29

HAVE SOME FUN

Business is serious but it need not be solemn. Even the best people can't achieve greatness if they're discouraged, bored, or scared.

Business people who believe that humor has no place in the workplace are probably threatened by the creativity it seems to generate. Humor is a natural catalyst for creativity because:

- Humor requires quickness of mind to generate.

- Humor helps to relax people; you can't be tense and laugh at the same time!

- Laughter releases those magic endorphins that lift spirits and aid ingenuity.

- A little levity provides a needed diversion from the routine.

A few good-natured laughs in the workplace can actually help improve performance. Good humor = good work.

ACTION STEPS

☐ Signal your appreciation for (or tolerance of) humor on the job. Join your staff in celebrating the lighter moments.

☐ Post an appropriate cartoon on occasion; encourage a few laughs at a meeting.

☐ Ensure that the laughs come at no one's expense (unless you make yourself the butt of your own jokes).

☐ _____

_____

_____

CHAPTER 30

TREAT EVERYONE WHO REPORTS TO YOU AS AN INDIVIDUAL

Too many organizations hire people who come equipped with brains and treat them like robots while teams of brilliant researchers spend untold millions working feverishly to teach robots to think like people!

As thinking and learning are individual processes, so is managing today's knowledge workers. Putting this ethic to work is often made much tougher by the way firms tend to smother individualism.

■ LIKE LIKES LIKE

Organizations strive for consistency in member behavior by enforcing rules that may be clearly codified or merely implied. Those expectations exert a powerful force for self-censorship of personal characteristics and thoughts that vary with the prescribed norm.

Consistency in dress, speech, hair styles, workspace decor, and the like—all in the name of nothing more valid than corporate sameness—stifles expression of individuality and independent thought. People walk through the company door and essentially agree to turn off their individuality in exchange for sufficient monetary payment.

People normally act within the expectations of their culture, so conformity becomes comforting. The system tends to reward employees—with raises, promotions, and special favors—who do more bootlicking than boat rocking.

▌ MANAGING INDIVIDUALS

People at work want to be treated as individuals, not as the workforce, troops, or labor. Treat each employee as a thinking, choice-making, competent person. As a manager, your job is to help an employee realize his or her personal potential which in turn helps your organization realize its potential.

A value-adding manager not only monitors and encourages everyone's good performance but also helps employees to discover and fulfill their ever-evolving potential. This emphasis on managing individuals is increasingly important as corporate hierarchies flatten.

When you concentrate on helping people fulfill their potential, your company will be filled not with workers but *craftsmen* who concentrate on making better wheels instead of feeling like cogs in one.

💡 ACTION STEPS

☐ Create in your corner of the organization a society where everyone is a colleague, some with more responsibility than others.

☐ Create a trusting environment where individual opinions and suggestions are not only permitted but requested.

☐ Give people the opportunity to explore, to try some new things, or try old things in new ways.

☐ Manage each person as an individual, not merely as a small part of a larger group. Make a point to be familiar with each person's résumé and personnel file.

What talents outside the job description and experiences outside your organization does each person bring to the job?

☐ Talk to your direct reports, and theirs, personally. Discuss, not announce. Listen.

☐ _____
_____
_____

Chapter 31

NOT NEGATIVE IS NOT POSITIVE

"If you don't hear from me, assume that you're doing a good job." You might have said something like that to your staff. You're busier than ever and you don't have time to give people much feedback. Besides, they should be working on their own; they're *empowered*. Right?

Don't you believe it. Telling people that they'll only hear from you when they've gone wayward isn't positive, liberating, or encouraging. Leave 'em alone management doesn't reinforce good performance and won't inspire greatness. To encourage employees to produce their best, most productive work, you've got to let them know that working that way matters more than just doing enough to keep you from chewing them out.

 ACTION STEPS

☐ Make a point to acknowledge good performance even if it's a conversation of only a few seconds or a note of a few words.

☐ When you give brief feedback, be sure you tell someone that a *specific* piece of work they did was the kind of contribution you really value, and tell them *why*. Examples:

    ☐ "Mary, your handling of the Jones file showed real imagination and professionalism. Your ingenious solution pleased our customer and kept us profitable on the account. Nice work."

"Susan, your design for that new process will cut our costs by about 3 percent with no loss of productivity. That's the kind of work that'll help us grow this year. Thanks!"

☐ _____

_____

_____

CHAPTER 32

WHAT'S IMPORTANT GETS BUDGETED

If you say you value increasing employee competence and recognizing good performance, your budget should speak as clearly as your words. While education and recognition don't necessarily require large investments, they cost something. Budget for them. If you don't, you've indicated their true value to you.

Budgets institutionalize, remind, and signal to all your commitment. Budgets *communicate*.

ACTION STEPS

☐ Allocate money for employee education and recognition.

☐ Estimate likely actual expenses. Alternatively, consider budgeting a fixed amount per employee. You can distribute the funds unequally, but the per person figure gives you a starting point.

☐ Tell your employees that you have earmarked money for enhancing skills and acknowledging achievement. Let them know the basis on which you intend to spend those funds.

☐ Spend the money wisely and regularly.

☐ _____

_____

_____

CHAPTER 33

EMBRACE PEOPLE WHO COLOR OUTSIDE THE LINES

"What if" are the first words of all progress. They are usually spoken by a special kind of person. Such people may work on your staff; you may be such a person yourself.

People willing to challenge convention are known by many names: pioneers, oddballs, rogues, gadflies, renegades, radicals, creatives, eccentrics, geniuses, heretics, individualists, dynamos, malcontents, and mavericks. Whatever the label, all progress depends on people who blaze new trails around, through, and over the old ones. To improve the system you must challenge it.

As a value-adding manager, you must encourage those who appoint themselves Champions of the Cause to Improve the Business. They look for ways to do new things and new ways to do old things. Risking repercussions from the powers that be, these mavericks wager their very livelihoods to do what they feel needs to be done, challenging, ignoring, or thwarting organizational policies all the way. Authority neither intimidates nor inhibits them. Such people need your guidance, your encouragement, and your patience.

ACTION STEPS

☐ Encourage the enthusiasm of people who chafe against the status quo.

☐ Focus your driven, imaginative employees. Help

Wilkie

them to bring their immense energy and creativity to bear against current priorities and challenges.

☐ Respond to suggestions for improvements in the organization by fairly evaluating suggestions and doing so in a timely fashion.

☐ If you can implement good ideas, do so and give credit to the courageous souls who put the ideas on the agenda. If you can't use the suggestions, explain why. Promise to keep the recommendations on file for future reference.

☐ Make clear that while you value creative enterprise, you must still hold your dynamos to performing well in their current responsibilities.

☐ _____

_____

_____

CHAPTER 34

GET 'EM TO KISS SOME FROGS

Not all intensely focused efforts will hit bull's-eyes. If you don't acknowledge admirable albeit unsuccessful efforts in a positive way, people soon come to understand that only successes have value. They'll self-censor any risk taking; which just about assures a safely mediocre place to work (until the company is driven out of business by innovative competitors).

At 3M, failures are acknowledged as stepping stones to success. A common saw around St. Paul: You've got to kiss a lot of frogs to find a prince. How can you acknowledge failures without appearing to encourage them? How about a Horseshoe Award (close counts!), or a College Try Award.

Give an account of how *you* failed in things you've tried and how that contributed to your own success. You're not displaying weakness but strength. Let people know that you value and identify with their brave attempt.

Everybody loves a winner, but most winners win by playing the odds; the more attempts, the more likely a success (familiar example: Edison's several hundred failures to find a workable filament for an incandescent light). Fewer attempts, less chance for success. Pay tribute to the valiant effort and encourage more of the same right away. If at first you don't succeed . . . ; Nothing ventured, nothing . . . ; The best thing to do after falling off a horse . . . ; No pain, no . . . ; When the going gets tough . . .

ACTION STEPS

☐ Encourage your employees to try more than the tried and proven.

☐ Communicate to them that you don't expect perfection and that mistakes made in good faith are not fatal.

☐ Dissect substandard results and insist that mistakes lead to new insights.

☐ _____

_____

_____

Chapter 35

Provide Visibility

Allow top performers to personally present to upper management a proposal or report of results for a program with which they're involved. Provide an opportunity to teach; an ego-gratifying exercise. The chance to make a presentation to peers, to educate junior team members, or to address a company conference can give an achiever a chance to strut his or her stuff.

If it is appropriate to your line of work, enter your people's products in a contest for design or quality. This communicates your pride in their achievements, underscores the value of laboring for the sake of merit and not merely compensation, and it reinforces the organization's mission to create competition-quality output.

Action Steps

☐ Identify opportunities to showcase a deserving person or team, seeking to match talents with an appropriate vehicle (not everyone is suited for or wants to make a presentation before the executive committee).

☐ Offer the recognition opportunity to the candidate and allow for an out with no penalty.

☐ Offer to help in any way you can to make sure this reward doesn't end up as a punishment.

☐ _____

_____

CHAPTER 36

ARRANGE FOR A SPECIAL ASSIGNMENT

Everyone has favorite work. Reward top performers with theirs. You might need to shuffle the workload temporarily, but you'll get the benefit of work that wouldn't ordinarily spring from the daily routine, and your top performers will get a chance to spread their wings.

A related alternative is to let someone try something new. All employees are adept at doing more than they were hired to do. By providing your capable people with a diversity of assignments, you'll find them becoming more diversely capable. Reward achievers by asking them what they'd like to tackle. Or, ask for volunteers. Give people a chance to surprise you with work out of the ordinary and they will.

ACTION STEPS

☐ Create an assignment that makes the most of an individual's special talents.

☐ Make clear that the special assignment is temporary (unless you're prepared for a more permanent shift of responsibilities); this is a perk, not the stuff of false hopes.

☐ Let people try something new. It breaks up the routine, transfers skills, and broadens the resources you have at your disposal.

☐ Seek volunteers for special projects.

☐ _____

_____

_____

CHAPTER 37

ENCOURAGE TIME AWAY FROM WORK

An acquaintance of mine gives a key staffer time off to pursue her fine art talents. She knows it motivates the employee more than money and requires no extra hit to cash flow.

Time away from work helps your hard workers recharge their batteries and exposes them to additional experiences that can help stimulate even more achievements in your organization.

Fran Tarkenton, management consultant and chairman of Knowledgeware, a successful computer software company, thinks time off is valuable for senior executives too. "Many corporate executives rarely take more than a week off. And during this week they have things faxed to them, they call their lawyers or bankers, and they never disconnect. As a result, they lose their perspective, and their capacity to regenerate and rejuvenate will vanish. I think that's very counterproductive."

Tarkenton puts his money where his mouth is. "I force my top executives to take one entire month off each year. They've got to take it, no matter what."

 ACTION STEPS

☐ Clearly communicate your expectation that your employees will use their available vacation and other days off.

☐ Monitor your employees' days off. If they aren't taking them, urge them or order them to do so.

☐ Use time off as a reward for extraordinary achievement.

☐ _____

_____

_____

Chapter 38

Provide Time to Pursue a Personal Project

As a matter of policy, 3M encourages its scientists to spend 15 percent of their time on projects that interest them, even if the projects are entirely unrelated to assigned work. That's an hour and 12 minutes out of an eight-hour day. That doesn't sound like much but if you saved the time to spend it in one day a week, it's a good chunk of the day.

The key to making this idea work is to really free the person to enjoy the time you claim to have provided. If you made such an offer to one of your people without relieving them of regular work expectations, the reward would amount to a cruel hoax.

Earning a 15 percent time bonus while still having to meet the same expectations, or doing everything that needed to be done before the award, means working more than another hour every day. Some treat! I admit to falling into this trap. Someone would come to me with an innovative idea. "Great!" I'd declare. "Go do it." But then I see that person struggle to juggle what already was a very full-time job with the pet project.

Sometimes you can't relieve a key person of routine responsibilities. Be honest about that. "I can't officially free you up to pursue that great idea, but I'd love to see you develop it if you want to." You might be surprised to see that person burning the midnight oil or working through the weekend on a labor of love, expecting no additional remuneration just for being encouraged to stretch.

When people demonstrate that they're good at doing something, let them do it. But don't take them for granted or ignore them.

💡 ACTION STEPS

- ☐ Encourage a top performer to pursue a personal project that holds promise for your organization.

- ☐ Set reasonable ground rules. Be brutally honest about whether you can lighten the official load the person normally carries.

- ☐ Establish an end time for the special allotment.

- ☐ Make clear that priority work takes precedence.

- ☐ _____

  _____

  _____

Chapter 39

Let Your Stars Moonlight

Rare is the person whose work meets all their psychic needs. Some modest after-hours professional endeavors, in accord with strict guidelines, can provide a refreshing diversion from the workplace and stimulating enrichment to bring back there. (My personnel file includes a letter of permission to give speeches; I sign a corporate code of conduct agreement every year specifying prohibitions against potential conflicts of interest.)

Action Steps

☐ Allow, perhaps encourage, your employees to seek broadening activities both within and outside the organization.

☐ Set clear guidelines about conflicts of interest and unacceptable use of your organization's assets for activities that do not benefit it.

☐ _____
_____
_____

CHAPTER 40

USE RECOGNITION SPARELY AND PURELY

Saying "thank you" to your employees using the recognition methods suggested in this book strikes some managers as frilly and silly. But a word to the most hard-core bottom-liner: This stuff works. It's not childish; however, these techniques tend to work best when you deal with employees as adults while appealing to the child that lies within.

Performance rewards aren't "feel good" freebies; and they aren't unbusinesslike. They keep people focused on organizational goals and achievement. Dispersing psychic paychecks should be treated as seriously as the fiscal kind. At the same time, psychic paychecks shouldn't be dangled before workers as a mule's carrot. They should not be promised, conditional, or bargained for, but be signs of genuine appreciation for accomplishment. The importance of this distinction can't be overstated.

Recognizing a job well done lets people know that their extraordinary efforts didn't go unnoticed even if undercompensated. It's as if you, the value-adding manager, are sharing in the *joy of creation* experienced in work exceptionally well done. Such recognition is feedback, not payment.

Simple gestures acknowledge extremely high-quality work and affirm the producer's rightful pride, which in moderation is a healthy and potent motivator. Pride, after all, simply means that people are happy with themselves for what they've accomplished. Taking pride in work well done encourages employees to make their next iterations even stronger.

Your employees should welcome your recognition but not expect it; awards are rewards not entitlements. You would do a disservice to your people to turn them into attention-craving praise junkies.

ACTION STEPS

☐ For greatest effect, vary motivational awards.

☐ Use recognition sparingly, wisely, and purely.

☐ _____

_____

_____

CHAPTER 41

FIGHT IGNORANCE: GET SMARTER

By undertaking a program of constant self-education, you'll become a more competent and successful manager. You can never know too much or all there is. The personal motto of Michelangelo is one we should all adopt: "I am still learning."

HOW TO LEARN IN THE OFFICE AND BEYOND

Rekindle your curiosity. Look for revelations and insights in all your activities and interactions. To learn from what you do, you need to be aware of and think about what you do.

Speak originally. When was the last time you actually wanted to kill two birds (or even one) with a stone? Is the expression relevant? How about "that was the last straw"?

Eliminate clichés from your conversations and writing. Clichés are verbal habits. They trap us in the rut of repeating others' expressions, some of which go back centuries and have no relevant analog in the modern world. Try creating your own metaphors. You'll draw on and improve your creative powers by forcing more of those important neural connections in your cranium, plus you'll add interest and impact to your communication. To paraphrase jazz great Thelonius Monk, sometimes you'll say things you never heard before.

Question. Becoming smarter is often as easy as asking

questions to which you don't know the answer—histori-cally a rare and courageous managerial act. If you want to get smarter about your operation, ask the people who run it—your employees. You will learn, your people will appre-ciate your interest, and they'll grow as well.

Not only should you ask questions of others, you might question yourself, most of all your truths. Beliefs, like logic, limit more than free. Maria Mitchell, 19th-century American astronomer wrote: "Besides learning to see, there is another art to be learned—not to see what is not."

Ask why. Ask why five times. Then twice more. This is a popular Japanese problem-solving method. An example: Your car stops abruptly. Why? It ran out of oil. Why? It hadn't been serviced. Why? You didn't get to it. Why? You've been too busy lately. Why? You've had to work much longer hours than normal. Why? Your workload seems much greater since the reorganization. Why? You've been reluctant to delegate. Why? You don't want to let go of certain tasks. Why? You're afraid your staff might actually be able to handle the responsibilities you reserved for yourself. Aha!

End every day with a question. What did you learn today? That reflection often will present you with new insights and teach you as much or more than any learning materials you could buy.

Invest in your brain. Tim Connor, president of TR Training Associates in Ann Arbor, Michigan, points out that most people spend hundreds of dollars every year on the outside of their heads (for hairstyling, makeup, fragrances, clothing) and thousands more on an automobile to transport themselves to work in high style. He asks, "What did you invest last year on the inside of your head so you would know what to say when you got there?"

You *don't* need to spend big bucks to get educated. You can learn from the very best material available for no cost at all. Renew your public library card and take advantage of a wealth of resources. Many colleges have a "friend of the library" program where you can check out materials for a modest fee, usually about the cost of one hardcover book.

Use idle time to learn more. Read while waiting in line. Caught without reading material? Strike up a conversation; everyone can teach you something (even if it's an appreciation for solitude). Read while you're vacationing. Read before falling asleep. Listen to informative tapes or broadcasts while commuting; more and more video stores rent audiotapes, and some companies will let you rent tapes by mail. Take 15 minutes out of every lunch hour to read and you'll gain more than an hour's worth of knowledge every week.

Don't savor the insignificant. Many people say they

don't have time to read the literature in their field, but they really mean they don't have time to read every word of those publications. Skim trade journals, look (with an open mind) at many competitive products, see as much of the landscape as possible. Then choose the items you wish to invest time absorbing. You'll know a little about a lot—so nothing should surprise you—and more about what's important.

"Chance favors only the mind that is prepared," advised Louis Pasteur, who was an artist as well as scientist. When you use the methods described above, you'll be prepared to come up with better ideas and make better decisions. Career growth in our new economy is not title inflation, it's expansion of the self through self-directed improvement.

⏻ ACTION STEPS

☐ Recognize what you don't know.

☐ Find out what you need to know; ask your employees for their insights.

☐ Eliminate clichés from your speech; you must think originally to speak that way.

☐ Ask questions—especially "why?"—to begin learning what you need to know.

☐ Set a quota for new ideas and record your ideas so that you can put them to work.

☐ Expose yourself on a regular basis to new information.

☐ Use your public library card or become a friend of a college library.

☐ Use your waiting time to improve yourself.

☐ Allow yourself to skim great quantities of information.

☐ _____

_____

_____

CHAPTER 42

PURSUE PRIME PERFORMANCE NOT PERFECTION

Are you a perfectionist? Because talented managers are highly capable people, some hold themselves to standards achievable only by a superman or superwoman: Stronger than all their colleagues, leaping tall problems in a single bound, thinking faster than a speeding bullet. All their lives, high achievers have heard that they are different, more capable, and specially gifted. That reputation, many believe, must be maintained at all costs.

Some extraordinary individuals develop an intolerance for imperfection in themselves and others. This condition, known as the perfection infection, can be especially pronounced in people who have been "winners" in their school, athletic, or business careers. "I am capable of perfection, therefore I must attain it," believes the unusually talented performer. Being wrong or failing isn't just disappointment, it's bad. As in "Bad boy!" or "Bad girl!" A missed deadline? A failed venture? Better to be hit by a truck. A sick day? What, the invincible man weakened? Impossible.

The German poet Johann Wolfgang von Goethe defined the perfectionist as someone "whom it is impossible to please because he is never pleased with himself." That pitiful condition is especially troubling when such a person occupies a management post. Then the fanaticism for perfection impacts not only the perfectionist but others, creating stress for all of them.

When in doubt, SuperExecutives postpone decisions and

demand more information. When they say, "It's your call"—
something they almost never say, buddy, you'd better be
right!

Proposals to perfectionist bosses are never good
enough. They can't be. If they were, SuperManagers would
lose their status. "What's wrong with it," you ask timidly.
"It's not thought out well enough," comes the intimidating
reply. Translation: My perfect power breakfast is giving me
indigestion beneath this perfect power suit; I'm the big
brain around here and don't you forget it!

This you're-never-right-no-matter-how-hard-you-try attitude leads to arbitrary and elusive standards. "You cut costs
5 percent? Well, that was just Phase One. I expect at least
another . . . "

"Perfect" bosses are unapproachable, especially about
the possible error of their own ways. After all, how does
one improve upon perfection? Someone possessed by the
perfection infection easily falls prey to paralysis by analy-
sis—avoiding risk which could mean failure which wouldn't
be perfect. "I think we'd better study this unproved strat-
egy/product/process a little further before going ahead
[after I retire]."

"Perfect" bosses are also known as "control freaks." The
compelling need to run a perfect—not competent, not excellent, *perfect*—operation, leads to megalomania.

Bosses suffering the perfection infection might be mistaken for workaholics. They are not. Workaholics mistake
compulsive, occasionally aimless, motion for productive
work. "Perfect" bosses truly are working on productive
matters that they are afraid to delegate to imperfect subordinates. And because they shoulder far more than their fair

share, perfect bosses will likely work themselves to a premature death.

Though "perfect" bosses may engage in counterproductive behavior, organizations tend to reward their dysfunction. Perfectionists appear to do everything right. Because they are so demanding, their operations perform to expectation (come hell or high water) so perfectionists collect their bonuses and receive their promotions.

If the perfectionist executive's unreasonable expectations drive out a few good junior managers, or if his or her highly competitive behavior—"I'm better than you, see!"—drives out a few colleagues, no matter. The perfectionist will bear the burden and work that much longer and harder.

In the long run, only perfectionists, their staff, and their organization suffer. Got it? Perfect.

ACTION STEPS

☐ Look in the mirror. Do you see a perfectionist? Lighten up. Laugh at yourself.

☐ Strive for quality, work up to high standards. Recognize and accept the gap between that and perfection.

☐ Let your staff know that you value great work but realize that achieving perfection in many tasks is simply not worth the effort required. Pick your spots.

☐ _____

_____

_____

_____

CHAPTER 43

LEADERSHIP IS INADEQUATE

Popular business literature celebrates the notion of leadership. Books and magazine articles promise to help you "find your leadership style," as though it were somehow lost. If you're looking to find leadership, better to adopt an ethic. Style will present itself.

Leaders in an organization, pundits suggest, prevail over management. They alone possess a compelling vision that points everyone in the right direction. Leaders decide and act while managers analyze and control.

Leadership is a perfectly good concept. Just about every organization needs more vision, principled decisions, and action. But leadership is not an inclusive model for the manager who wants to encourage innovation and active participation by everyone. Here's why. By definition, leaders need followers. The head leading the hands. The thinker leading the doers.

E. V. "Rick" Goings, president of Avon, articulates the proper balance between establishing a vision for a firm and enabling everyone in it to pursue that vision. "My job is to (1) set the vision for the company—it's not a committee decision, and then, (2) share that vision with all the people in the corporation so that they are mobilized to fully invest themselves in fulfilling it."

Rick Goings gracefully dances along the tightwire on which many executives fear to set foot, the one strung between controlling employees and process at the one end, and freeing workers to do what they think needs to be done to fulfill the corporate mission at the other. Goings is saying: Here's where we're going, you get there by the route and means you think are best. With the corporate mission clearly defined, employees are free to improve the business through their creativity. Goings points people toward a goal, but he doesn't ask them to follow him there while staring at his backside.

One need not be a CEO like Rick Goings to make such an ideal a reality. No matter where you are on the organization chart, you face this tightwire within the arena of your own responsibility. Master the skills to walk that wire with aplomb or fall fast and hard.

 ACTION STEPS

☐ Recognize that choosing between being a manager or being a leader is a false dichotomy. As an effective boss you'll lead occasionally, manage occasionally, and always involve the people for whom you take responsibility.

☐ Give people a clear idea of where you'd like them to take the organization. Let them devise their own ways of getting there, provided they do so within clear standards for quality and limits for budget.

☐ _____

_____

_____

Chapter 44

Use the Annual Review to Look in the Mirror

When it's time for you to conduct the dreaded annual performance review for a member of your staff, take turns. Well in advance of the scheduled review, ask the employee to review his or her own performance. Then ask the employee to review your performance and that of the department. What improvements could be made and inefficiencies eliminated? Are you accessible, knowledgeable, supportive? Are you open to new ideas and differing points of view? Do you value initiative? Do you give credit where credit is due?

Even better, don't wait for the annual review. Inquire more frequently. Start today.

 Action Steps

☐ Communicate to your staff that you expect them to review your performance.

☐ Create a simple review for your employees to complete. For the most candid look in the mirror, let them complete it anonymously.

☐ At a minimum, use an employee's annual review as an occasion to get a reading on your own performance. Ideally, you should be reviewing your employees' performance—and seeking their opinion on yours—far more frequently than annually.

☐ _____

_____

_____

CHAPTER 45

MAKE A HABIT OF BREAKING HABITS

You're successful because you've developed and make a habit of using successful methods that work for you. But be warned: Habits, even good ones, put you into a rut.

Habits confine you. Doing things differently may actually effect a physical change in your brain. While research on the brain reveals new information all the time, it appears that our actions relate to connections between certain cells in our brains.

When you act out of the ordinary, you may create new neural patterns. Just as you can change the performance of a bicep by exercising it, you may physically alter your brain patterns to improve its performance. New actions influence new thinking. Think of breaking habits not only as exercise for your brain but also as a great way to see the world afresh.

Here are some habit breakers. Try going up steps with your right foot first instead of your left. Change the route you take to work. Change the hours you work. Eat lunch with someone you haven't eaten lunch with before. Eat lunch alone. Put on your jacket using your left arm first instead of your right arm. If you don't exercise, try it; if you do, change the routine. Read a section of the paper you never read. Listen to a radio station you never tune in and may not even like. Visit a restaurant you never tried before and order something you've never heard of before. Call an acquaintance you haven't spoken to in years. Brush your teeth with the hand you normally don't use to do that.

Break (politely) an obligation. Commit yourself to something you've been avoiding. Read a novel. Read a joke book. Buy a book for a friend. Go away with your significant other for a weekend. Give up drinking alcohol or eating dessert for a week. Volunteer for a charity. Play a sport you've never tried. Use your other ear to listen to the phone. Take a long, slow walk around your neighborhood, trying to see it for the first time. Find some fresh flowers to smell; close your eyes and savor the aroma. If you can't remember jokes, commit two to memory. Throw a party. Stay home and do nothing one weekend. Seek and spend time with someone significantly older than you, then someone significantly younger. Buy a crossword puzzle book and do at least half the puzzles. Send a romantic card to your spouse; read as many cards as you can before selecting one, especially the funny ones. Watch something on public television for which the listing sounds as dull as flat paint. Watch a raucous game show. Switch brands of toothpaste. Observe a stranger and try to imagine his or her life story. Take a class unrelated to work or your hobbies—how about cultural anthropology or physics? Reserve time to spend with your children or someone else's children; they'll appreciate that more than you can know, and you'll get back in touch with your childlike self.

Throw open new windows to your mind. Clear out the mental cobwebs. Surprise yourself.

 ACTION STEPS

☐ Make a list of actions you make habitually.

☐ Make a habit of using habit substitutes.

☐ Enjoy the discomfort you'll feel when you first break habits. It will soon turn into an exciting sense of liberation.

☐ _____

_____

_____

CHAPTER 46

DON'T MANAGE BY BUZZWORD

As surely as you are in the midst of reengineering and trying to empower your people, business buzzwords inevitably erupt to describe the latest management fad.

This tendency is not new. Since the Industrial Revolution gave rise to the division of labor, people have struggled to find metaphors for their approach to managing the people who produce the work. The metaphor for effectively managing people today is not stick, not carrot, not stopwatch. If we *had* to have such a metaphor, it might be *training wheel*: helping people by initially working closely with them, then freeing them to go solo to an agreed upon destination by whatever reasonable route they choose.

Good management is not packaged or labeled. Your employees won't work any smarter, harder, or happier because you utter faddish phrases.

 ACTION STEPS

☐ Stay current on the latest management concepts. But just as you wouldn't rush to buy a leisure suit or bellbottoms, don't mindlessly repeat trendy buzzwords— or worse, try to manage by them.

☐ Before you let a voguish slogan fall from your lips, ask yourself: "What does this mean? Do I clearly understand it? Will my employees and colleagues understand it to mean the same thing? Have I changed the way I manage or merely my terminology?"

☐ _____

_____

_____

CHAPTER 47

WELCOME DISAGREEMENT

A fascinating proposal for change was put on the table at a recent meeting. After advancing the concept, its author—a competent, secure manager—concluded by announcing in a small voice, "It's just a thought." That hedge, that implied declaration of an apology for an idea that might offend the status quo, bothered me greatly.

Does your organization suffer from the nice-ification of the workplace? Do you work in a sterile, play-up-to-the-boss, phony "have a nice day" environment? Constant agreement lacks energy, creativity, and life. The English poet Lord Byron wrote, "Adversity is the first path to truth."

Sameness of thought yields neither passion nor progress. Friction can generate the spark of a new idea (the word *conflict* derives from a Latin term meaning "to strike together") creating an energy that well-intending colleagues can positively direct to problem solving. Sweet and sour make for a tasty meal. Contrary-smelling substances such as skunk oil and flowers commonly make perfume. In the same way, ideas in opposition bumping against one another can give rise to totally new ideas. Diversity is better than uniformity.

AGREE TO DISAGREE

Emotion, conviction, and intensity all show that one cares about the business, not that one lacks team spirit. Team-work doesn't mean compliant submission to harmonious,

109

bureaucratic mediocrity. Some of the most creatively productive meetings in which I've participated gave birth to new ideas amid raised voices, table pounding, and displays of naked emotion. You need not fight to progress but you must avoid avoidance of conflict.

Disagreements in the work place need not be win or lose contests between people. Conflict is only energy. Energy comes from polarity; what good is a battery with only a positive terminal? Isn't it interesting that our most familiar symbols for creativity are the lightning bolt and the lightbulb. The lightning bolt is created by the clash of opposite electrical charges; the energy for the lightbulb is produced in the same fashion.

▌ CONSIDERATIONS FOR CONSTRUCTIVE CONFLICT

1. No-holds-barred discussions should be encouraged only between a small number of people with equivalent organizational status where no one holds the power of retribution over another. What is more inhibiting to the free exchange of ideas than for a boss to call together all his or

her direct reports for an idea session only to announce, "Here's what I think. Now what do you think?"

2. Passionate discussions should always focus on issues, *never* on people. A business associate of mine laments "think-tank" meetings with other executives in his company. "The real problem occurs when two of the superachievers get into a room together and start talking about important issues. In no time, they're at each other's throats, battling for position. By the end of the meeting, there's blood on the floor." A properly run meeting should never allow that to happen.

3. Open discussions probably work best when chaired by an outsider with no allegiance to any proposition or faction. It may work best when the moderator has an entirely fresh perspective outside the shared assumptions of people in the company or even industry. If the facilitator isn't an outsider, he or she should be someone who can function with no fear of political consequences, and someone whose unique personal experience brings a dimension to the questions before the group which it wouldn't otherwise have.

The mediator should keep the focus on exploring possibilities, not defending positions. Personal rivalries or animosities that arise during the discussion should be directed away from participants and toward the problem at hand.

4. Everyone at the session should participate. The moderator should draw out more reticent participants; the discussion is not an exercise solely for the brave or vocal. A technique some group leaders use is known as the Talking Stick or the Conversation Ball. The stick or ball is handed to the person talking. This visible sign of dominance makes each speaker aware of exactly how much time he or she is in control of the dialogue. It also assists in controlling the

decorum of the discussion, reminding participants that the most benefit is achieved by listening to one speaker at a time.

5. To fully exploit the creative possibilities in the session, all avenues of thought—even sensitive areas—should be explored without reservation. Irrelevant or bizarre ideas stimulate fresh thinking and often provoke laughter. Levity and frivolity catalyze more connections and combinations that can lead to striking insights.

A value-adding manager knows that people can express unconventional ideas, question policies, and differ with the boss without threatening management's authority. Disagreements and arguments with colleagues don't represent a breakdown in organizational integrity. On the contrary, earnest dissent is a sign of trust and respect. The most compliant environments often represent the most disharmonious and dysfunctional.

 ACTION STEPS

☐ Examine your own views toward conflict. When was the last time you invited challenge or at least a frank appraisal of your policies and methods?

☐ Orchestrate dissent. Put a taboo subject on a meeting agenda; that will get a group to discuss it without fear of reprisal. Rather than leaping into a sensitive subject, work up to it by first dealing with more mundane matters.

☐ Hold an even-handed debate. Encourage factions at odds over a controversial proposal to debate the proposition before their colleagues. Here's the twist:

Each side must come prepared not only to present its case but also that of the other school(s) of thought. Thus, everyone must thoroughly think through all the positions, advancing their best thinking on all possibilities. A postdebate discussion led by an independent moderator may yield an improved or entirely new approach to the question on the table.

☐ Solicit ideas via silent ballot. A venerable method for raising unpopular notions involves collecting anonymous contributions from interested participants. Specific methods vary but practitioners of this process generally write their controversial suggestions (or reactions to such a proposal) on cards or slips of papers. A moderator collects the tickets, sorts them, and frames additional discussion to which the participants again react.

☐ _____

_____

_____

CHAPTER 48

CARRY A PROBLEM AROUND

The Latin root of the word *ponder* means weight. An unresolved challenge or postponed decision on an opportunity weighs heavily upon the mind. The burden can make one tense and grumpy.

One of the reasons many people seize the first possible solution to a problem is to relieve themselves of the anxiety of dragging around a problem in the subconscious all day. Inspired solutions often bubble up after the difficult problem has stewed in the mind a long time. Endure the strain of living with a problem until it's fully decomposed by your brain's digestive juices.

ACTION STEPS

☐ Carry your problems around longer than you'd like; you'll reward yourself with brilliance born of considerable contemplation.

☐ _____
_____
_____

CHAPTER 49

MEET YOUR IDEA QUOTA

One of the best ways to have great ideas is to have many ideas. Assign yourself a quota. Starting with just two ideas a day, you'll accumulate more than 700 per year. In a decade, that's over 7,000 ideas.

The ideas you write down need not come from trying to think of ideas. In fact, trying to call forth ideas seems to sometimes scare them away. Ideas can come from things you hear or overhear, or see in the paper, along the roadside, on television, or in your dreams. The point is to get into the routine of capturing concepts that captivate you.

The more adept you get at thinking skills, the more adept your thinking becomes. Soon you'll become prolific. As the task of finding or coming up with ideas gets easier and easier, the quality of your ideas tends to improve as well.

 ACTION STEPS

☐ Always carry a device for capturing your fleeting thoughts. A thought unwritten is an idea lost. Pencil and notebook, a tape recorder; 3-by-5-inch note cards—all make for a great traveling database. The proverbial pen and pad of paper on the nightstand is a good idea. (Waterproof pad for the shower?)

☐ Collect the ideas in a notebook or file drawer, always in the same place. Categorize them if you wish, but that's not necessary. What is important is to review them periodically. You might find that you previously came up with a solution to a problem that you just started experiencing, or conceived an opportunity that was slightly ahead of its time until now.

☐ Think multidimensionally about the ideas you record. Ask what the possible immediate consequences of these ideas are, for yourself and for others? What are the possible longer term consequences? Where else might these ideas lead?

☐ _____

_____

_____

CHAPTER 50

TRUST YOUR GUT

To open yourself up to insight, release yourself from the restrictions of reason. Some people escape from reason's confines with great difficulty (unless they're lost on a dark, stormy night and happen by a cemetery). Intuition is cultivated by use; it correlates to self-trust. Give in to your gut instincts.

Experience, true feelings, and hopes all speak quietly through the intuitive voice within. When that voice is a trusted friend, it can be a most powerful counselor.

ACTION STEPS

☐ Record your first instinct when wrestling with a tough decision. Chances are, you will gather data and try to reach a reasoned decision. You should at least know what your gut told you before your head overwhelms the decision-making process.

☐ When there's a conflict between head and gut, go with your gut.

☐ _____

_____

_____

CHAPTER 51

LIVE FOR MORE THAN DAILY BREAD

That quiet inner voice that gives you your best ideas can often come forward only when you block out the din of other stimuli. Our busy, plugged-in, megawatt/gigabit world seduces our attention ever so easily. Learn to shut it off.

If you don't reflect on what you've experienced, you can take no meaning from it. When you shut out the noise of the world, your mind will fill the sensory void with productive and sometimes amusing or even startling thoughts.

THINK ON THE GO

Use commuting time as meditating time. Video producer Steve Eiffert refers to his car as a "self-contained meditation unit." When you drive with the radio off, your mind can wander. When it wanders into some productive thinking, pick up the tape recorder. Talk out loud to yourself in the car. Dialogue with yourself is a great idea starter and tension reliever, and much cheaper than a therapist.

Don't drive? Not a problem. Reflect while commuting to work via train or bus. When my colleague Mary Gentle gets ideas while riding the rails, she describes the experience as a "trainstorm."

THE POWER OF SOLITUDE

Most businesses don't provide quiet places for people to reflect, but you might scout an empty office, an unused cubicle, a quiet corner in the cafeteria, or other refuge for stealing a few moments of quiet during the workday. This can help you clear your head of the many interruptions and distractions around your normal work area.

Your creativity productivity will increase as you grow accustomed to listening to your own thoughts. The more you're in touch with your innermost thoughts, the more you'll find them breaking through the noise of the daily routine with solutions to the challenges that confront you.

SEEK BALANCE

Humans do not walk the earth only to produce and sell widgets. Volunteering your substantial talents to worthy causes puts you in touch with people, experiences, and a part of yourself you might otherwise not encounter. Try to do charitable work in which you don't have a leadership role such as holding an office, but are just lending a hand. This humbler giving will fill a different part of you.

Every day do some chuckling, grinning, guffawing, smiling, cheering, winking, and giggling. Clip and post cartoons. Put four boxes on your desk, mark them: In, Out, Too Hard, Beats the Hell Out of Me. Seek levity in gravity.

I can't carry a tune, but I find they carry me. Music expresses and induces emotion. Most of our waking hours are spent keeping our emotions in check; music frees them.

Rediscover a long lost interest. Paint; play a sport; pick up that old guitar, clarinet, or camera.

Indulge, it's therapy.

ACTION STEPS

☐ Find solace every day. In the midst of your hectic life, find time to listen to silence.

☐ Record your thoughts.

☐ Volunteer to help a worthy cause.

☐ Look for humor and take time to laugh.

☐ Broaden yourself by sampling music of the world and experience the rhythms that move people around the globe.

☐ Rekindle or start a hobby to balance your life.

☐ _____

_____

_____

CHAPTER 52

YOUR PERSONALITY IS COMPETENCE

All business is simply human relationships involving money. In today's information/service economy, human contact prevails over less intimate transactions—not only with customers but inside the organization.

Historically, workers were subordinates in every respect, but today's skilled employees have radically different expectations. To be an effective value-adding manager, you must understand and be a sterling example of how to handle human interactions deftly by building positive, mutually respectful relationships with your staff. In today's smart, savvy and sophisticated workforce, managing your personality is competence.

ASSUMING RESPONSIBILITY

Would your staff hire you as a boss? Management is not about winning a popularity contest but about vision, fairness, and equitable treatment of those whose on-the-job behavior you would influence.

Good managers close the gap between the current reality and the corporate objective by moving to the destination alongside their charges—not in front of them, not pushing from behind, and not calling the plays from the isolation of a well-appointed office. The value-adding manager takes responsibility for results while enabling others to think and act innovatively to achieve shared goals.

All leaders, Napoleon contended, are determined by the led. **You can lead people only as far as they trust you to take them.**

💡 ACTION STEPS

☐ Recognize that your real authority to influence your employees comes more from them than from your employer.

☐ Study the basics of human psychology.

☐ Strive more to be a decent human being in your dealings with your staff than an embodiment of the latest techniques in management.

☐ _____
_____
_____

Don Blohowiak is a marketing executive in a successfully downsized unit of the Times Mirror Co. Now based in New York City, he has held management posts in southern California, Denver, Detroit, and Milwaukee. He faces daily the very pressures and challenges he addresses in this book, his third.

His widely acclaimed book *Mavericks!* has so far been translated into German, Portuguese and Hebrew.

He has been interviewed or cited by media as diverse as *USA Today Sky Radio*; Voice of America; Associated Press Radio Network; *NewsDay*, Business Radio Network; *Sonny Bloch's Business Journal*; Independent Broadcasting Network; *Library Journal*; *Signs of the Times*; *U.S. 1*; talk radio stations from Providence, Rhode Island, to Honolulu, Hawaii; *The American Entrepreneur*; Independent Radio Producers Network; daily newspapers from New York to California including the *New York Times* and *The Wall Street Journal*.

A provocative and entertaining public speaker, Don counts many associations and corporations as clients including Prudential Insurance, Dow Jones, and Exxon. He is represented by JR Associates in Princeton, NJ (609/921-6605).

You can contact Don at Box 791 Princeton Jct., NJ 08550-0791, or via the Internet at 76016.1446@compuserve.com.

Thank you for choosing Irwin Professional Publishing for your business information needs. If you are part of a corporation, professional association, or government agency, consider our newest option: Irwin Professional Custom Publishing. This allows you to create customized books, manuals, and other materials from your organization's resources, select chapters of our books, or both.

Irwin Professional Publishing books are also excellent resources for training/educational programs, premiums, and incentives. For information on volume discounts or Custom Publishing, call 1-800-634-3966.

Other books of interest to you from Irwin Professional Publishing . . .

The Wow Factory
Creating a Customer Focus Revolution in Your Business
Paul Levesque

Transcending the concept of customer *service*, this eye-opening book introduces Customer Focus as a corporate state of mind that has a direct bearing on the decisions that every person in the organization will make, every day.

0-7863-0386-7   192 pages

Empowering Employees Through Delegation
Robert B. Nelson
(Briefcase Books)

Shows you how—along with what and when—to delegate effectively. Will take the manager step-by-step through the process of delegating by communicating responsibility in a way that ensures all parties know exactly what is expected of them.

1-55623-847-9   175 pages